My Hyacinth Mountain

Antonino Monti

No Frills
<<<>>>
Buffalo
Buffalo, NY

Copyright © 2014 Antonino Monti

Printed in the United States of America

Monti, Antonino

My Hyacinth Mountain/ Albert- 1st Edition

ISBN: 978-0991045570

1. My Hyacinth Mountain – Poetry– Verse.
No Frills.
1. Title

No part of this book may be reproduced or transmitted in any form by any means, electronic or mechanical, including photocopying, recording, or by any information storage and retrieval system without permission in writing by the author.

No Frills Buffalo
119 Dorchester Buffalo, New York 14213
For more information visit
Nofrillsbuffalo.com

I'd like to dedicate this book to everyone that has touched my life past, present and future. I'd like to thank my mom, dad and sister and to my editor Alyssa.

A note from the author

I would like to take this chance to introduce myself, my name is Antonino Monti. I put this book together to give people a chance to look into my mind. The title has a special meaning to me because my name in latin means "Flower on a Mountain". So in turn this book is an extension of myself. I use poetry to release my inner most thoughts, the good, the bad, and the ugly. I write about life, death and the beauty in between. Thank you and I hope you enjoy.

Contents

My Resignation	*8*
Heaven	*9*
Lavender Fields	*11*
The White Curtain	*12*
Hyacinth Mountain	*13*
The Light	*16*
Plastic Universe	*17*
Mr. Brown	*19*
The Samurai	*21*
The King	*25*
The Life Force	*27*
The Question	*28*
The Devil and The Girl	*29*
Sophia	*31*
The Wise	*33*
I Dare	*36*
Jerry	*37*
The Abyss	*40*
Inspiration	*43*
The Disease	*45*
Never Ending Day	*46*
My Hair	*47*
No Disguise	*48*
They	*49*
The Queen	*51*

My Resignation

Let me tell you my friend,
that this is the end.
No time to pretend,
because this is the end.
Trapped in the snare of education,
rope pulling tight, I'm stuck on probation.

I can't believe what I've become,
I'm just a few from done.
This life has lost it's fun,
I'm waiting for the sun,
but the night has only begun.

I'm dead inside.
I've reached the end of my rope,
and there's nowhere to hide.
I'm an incompetent fool,
who sits on the side.
All I want to do is ride.

The long lie of your love,
sits idly in my mind,
but you are something I will never find.
This is an endless grind,
I think it's my time.

I can't believe what I've become,
I'm just a few from done.
This life has lost it's fun,
I'm waiting for the sun,
but the night has only begun.

Heaven

There's a place we all know,
in the depths of our minds,
where life meets death,
and the world begins to unwind,

The further you look inward,
the farther the sky expands,
gaze up, see the stars,
and grab them with your hands,

The universe is a pool of life,
with no real beginning or end,
you are everything that surrounds you,
because everything is your friend,

Close your eyes and you will see,
what this world is meant to be,
we all have to live for you and me,
but what is this world,
just a constant fight for we,

Reaching out for the stars,
this life we live sets the bar,
never again will I see the mar,
and heaven just seems so far.

Look around and see your brother,
he comes from another mother,
our bond with this world is like no
other,
because she is our true lover,

Just reach out for heaven,
reach is far as you can,
we are almost there,
do you see that man?
He's standing on the edge of heaven,

Reaching out for the stars,
this life we live sets the bar,
never again will I see the mar,
and heaven just seems so far.

Lavender Fields

Bursting open,
the gates with flood,
the levee is broken,
and there is nowhere to run.

The hero rises,
I will take you onward,
He says to the people.
we march on toward the Church's
steeple.

Back door mushroom man,
guides us through the endless fields of
lavender,
the world is bending on forever after.

Over the horizon floats a ship,
flags flown high of the led,
it twas but a zeppelin.

Elephants walk a straight path,
puffs of smoke rise with a laugh.
Pines surrounding, pillow of gold,
the world is everlasting and bold.

Spinning ball of energy lies,
in the depths of our souls,
to help us carry life's tolls.

Back door mushroom man,
guides us through the endless fields of
lavender,
the world is bending on forever after.

The White Curtain

We are children of the moon,
dance until the morning draws soon.
A white blanket covers the ground,
But who dares to look around.

A white curtain blocks my window,
I'm locked inside from this storm,
but I can hear the wind howl,
and the fire burns to keep me warm.

The greatest beauty keeps us inside,
we are so afraid that we hide.
No one wants to embrace it,
only sit back and waste it.

I want to leave my sacred place,
and embrace the rolling serenity,
it calls me past the white curtain,
there is no other place I'd rather be.

The icy chills can warm my heart,
I'll freeze away until the end of days,
when the eye comes and floats above my head,
I'll know that this path is the right way.

Run through the white curtain if you dare,
but leave behind all of your wears.
You don't need them in the place I roam,
because it is your true home.

Hyacinth Mountain

Trees garnish mountains,
on a quest for the fountain.
Life forever lasting,
no more will we be fasting.

Lead me down the path,
so that I may have a laugh.
Because life isn't so bold,
when your heart is cold.
Wisdom crowds the mind,
so you never know what you'll find.

Dragon sunrise,
fire fly high,
clouds ride by.
Soaring on the back,
there is nothing that I lack.

Castle walls are done,
I've but had my fun.
The kingdom flees, as the dragon flies low,
this might be the final blow.
A blaze higher than the trees,
It's a sight for all to see.

Mighty hero rises to the challenge,
for the kiss of Miss Lady he must win,
life without her is but a sin.
Drawing a sword from the ground,
the hero begins to look around.

Dragon comes back for another try,
only to be stopped by the sword in the sky.
The village burns no more,
and the hero stands at Miss Lady's door.

But a kiss is what I miss,
A love so strong and bold,
baby, baby,
this is old.
You make me feel so cold,
when your words are anything but bold.

Let me lead you down the path,
so that I may have a laugh.
Because life isn't so bold,
when your heart is cold.
Wisdom crowds the mind,
so you never know what you'll find.

Angel floats down on a cloud,
hero rides through the night,
they will meet in a grove of lilies,
unless he is stopped by the dark knight.

A battle will be waged,
if the hero is stopped tonight.
He rides at the ready,
hand on his sword,
ready for a fight.

Like two comets on a warpath,
their collision will create a great light.
The final test is coming soon,
and the world will see all his might.

Let me lead you down the path,
so that I may have a laugh.
Because this life isn't so bold,
when your heart is so damn cold.
Wisdom crowds the dark mind,
so you never know what you'll find.

This is my final say,
this is my last day.
The ship is leaving the harbor,
in the distance it moves farther.
A calm sea waits for their return,
as I sit here and burn.

The world is spinning onward now,
no where to run,
no where to hide,
laying down on my side.
I'm beside the fountain,
do you understand my Hyacinth
Mountain?

The Light

Darts on a board,
trinkets on a shelf.
Record spinning,
demon screaming.
Crate, carpet, floor,
protector and lover.
Twinkling lights,
ever so bright.
See the world,
through endless light.

Plastic Universe

Mist rides over the finger tip,
into the unknown.
Windows open,
in comes the breeze.
Brace yourself now, the train is drawing
close.
Plastic Universe sitting on a dollar bill,
my day goes on lifeless, without a thrill.

Safer to run now girl,
the world sits back.
The chase is over,
lets run.
The chase is over,
lets run.
Lets run.

A window before you stands,
never before has life been in man's
hands.
You're all just fools,
pawns in a game of chess,
your life means no more than the rest.

The people who rule you,
destroy you.
They only see the world from the eyes
of a few.
Take the throne,
thrash the castle,
the power can be ours with little hassle.

Rise! The throne is ours.
Rise! We'll be there in a few of hours.
Rise! Rise!
Demise! Demise!
No more lies,

say your goodbyes.
This is the end where everyone dies.
Rise!
Rise!

Mr. Brown

Walking across the ivy filled road,
searching for the wise and the old.
Waiting for a mystical tale,
to be told about an endless trial.
The young gather around,
as the music begins to fill the town.
A man appears on stage,
and the crowd is filled with rage.
But when the man creates a sound,
silence cloaks the ground.

The story begins,
with a man filled with sin.
He lives across town,
with a woman, Ms. Brown.

He cheats on his wife,
to add excitement to his life.
Steals from the poor,
to pay his fee at the door.
Sold his wife's locket,
to put money in his pocket.
Spends it on beer,
so he can hear himself cheer
about his sinful life,
until he has no wife.
When Ms. Brown realizes,
she's the most beautiful girl in town.

The man walks off stage,
his tale is done,
the crowd is better aged,
filled with a sense that they've won.

A guitar wails, as the lights go down.
The crowd recedes, and
the man hopes they'll follow his lead,

avoid a life of sin,
so in the end they can all win.

The Samurai

The sword flies high above his head,
the samurai knows only the dead.
His double edged sword fights for good,
as he trains in the woods.

Know not where I float now,
I stand before evil and refuse to bow.
Battle to the death this may be,
because the samurai know not how to flee.

He is a victim of his own home,
in this life he must stand alone.
Fighting with courage he will die,
so he can live forever in the sky.

Oh great samurai of my mind,
let me relax and unwind.
I know deep down I can find,
why you are ever present in my mind.

The fair maiden is traveling down the street,
her dress is a tapestry of red and blue.
It waves in the wind and revels her feet,
she is standing on a hilltop covered in dew.

A horseman approaches on his mighty stead,
the pyramid in his eyes, as he thinks of his deed.
The grass parts for him, for he is one of tree.

Around his necklace dangles a pendant
just like me.
A ship approaches over the horizon
riding a wave,
the face flies high bringing joy to all
those who see.
No one knows the captain's real name,
only Dave.
His face was stolen by the man of tree.

The two meet on an island of ice,
to trade tales of their deeds.
Everyday is a day of chance and a roll of
the dice,
and when their day comes they will
forever rest in the weeds,
For they have done a good deed.

Tree on fire,
calls for peace,
just a live wire,
coated in grease.
Record spinning,
notes floating,
music singing,
ears eroding.
Blue looks red,
white looks black,
colors are twisted,
no time to look back.
Great gates ahead,
pillows await,
the names are read,
all but red.

Endless skies of blue and grey,
today seems like the perfect day.
What else to do but sit and stare,
at the beautiful maiden, so elegant and fair.

Camouflage skeleton,
present on the table.
My dreams are so confusing,
they need no label.

Life's but one big mirage,
bountiful oasis.
I need to hurry up, and
chase this.

Life's confusing, hard to balance,
man is nothing without the mother,
for reliance and guidance.

Lost in my mind,
exploring the dreams I find.
Skyline of rainbow and awe,
impossible flaw.

A warm breath,
flows through the grass,
the scent of death,
lingers in my glass.
Drink,
I think,
one last blink,
as I sink,
down below.

Night is falling and all the people are beginning to arrive.
The moon brings forth an ominous glow,
the crowd surrounds the brewing fire.
Starring into it one sees a lost love.
Vengeful.
Lashing out,
leaping out of the fire.
Among mortals now,
chasing the one and only one.
One and one alone shall know the crime.
The fire tells no lie.

Ribbons of yellow and red,
stretch over the horizon, the sky is being fed.
Life is an endless death,
everyday is but one more breath.

Angel standing in a ring of roses,
come out and play,
we can spend a day,
exploring the lands over yonder.

The King

The king stands tall beside his throne,
as the choir begins to arrive,
there is fear in his face,
because they all know.

He can't sing,
so no one speaks to the king.
He can't sing,
as the bells begin to ring.
No the king can't sing,

He opens his mouth as if to release a shout,
but nothing echoes through the hall.
His family turns,
they're all ashamed,
the lion fails to roar.

I hear inside his heart the beating of a drum,
but he can't sing unless he drinks from the sacred rum.

Oh he can't sing.
No the king can't sing,
but the bells still ring.
And no one speaks to the king.

They think he's dumb,
as he approaches the rum.
His power can finally be shown,
but wait the king hears a ring.
To drink the whole thing,
and the people yell no.

The king is dead,
the shame went to his head.

He drank all he could,
in hopes that he could finally sing,
but still no one speaks to the king,
and the bells continue to ring,
oh they ring.
For the loss of a dear king,
too bad he couldn't sing.

The Life Force

Echoes on a walk,
they walk beside me,
in the shadows they call home.
Distant, waiting, watching.
Movement can show,
they are planning, ever so slightly.
Breeze on the rooftops,
nearly silent.
They recite a prose,
life questioning altar, life everlasting.
Blood is drawn to the mind,
everywhere,
bleeding, stop.
Where are you going?
Don't leave now, your time is almost
through.
The gates will be open soon,
messengers in the dark shadows,
ominous, life enthralling.
Death constantly waiting,
one slip and we break through.
Darkness, evermore.
New eternal, painless,
life,
death,
no difference, one in the same.
One is crucial for the other,
An eternal torch moving,
through generations,
eternities.
The life force.

The Question

Mist in a valley,
parts to the moons glow.
Night crawlers walking,
the world begins to show,
a life of everlasting,
eternity,
the spirit moves onward.
Choose between the paths,
morning sun draws near.
Colors rain from above,
the dream is over,
as you fall asleep.

Along the river we walk,
death leads, I follow.
Holding a scythe,
he leads me to a cliff.
This is the world,
mortal and immortal.
You must choose a portal,
enjoy life's bliss and sorrow,
or live a forever tomorrow.

The dream begins,
and the sun rises.
Warriors covered in decorative medals,
driving the car he can't reach the pedals.
Full throttle onward,
we can't go much faster,
there's no looking past her.
The judge guards the door,
and no one speaks to the king,
no one speaks to the king.

The Devil and the Girl

The Devil walks through the front door,
and says to the girl, "Your life is no more".
She pleads with the Devil, "Why me?"
"there are plenty worse people can't you see?"

"But you are who I'm after", says the Devil,
"Your life is over, time to start a new level."
"Follow me into the fire so you can be reborn,"
"and one day loved and adorn."

Every time you curse the world for what it gives you,
remember that some things in life are only good for a few.
You're not the only one on this Earth,
so make your life something with worth.

The Devil walks through the front door,
and says to the girl, "your life is no more."
But at least now she can understand,
that this world has a greater plan.

Like night she rides by candle light,
as the moon shines bright.
Like night she shines bright,
as the moon rides by candle light.

The world around me doesn't always
feel so right,
but I know I just have to make it to the
morning light.
There's only one way to fight,
to save the morning light.

Ocean breeze at it's height,
gonna make me feel so right.
Climb the mountain, fly by night,
run until you see the morning light.

Sophia

She comes from Peru,
and all I want to do,
is say hi.

Angel sitting next to me,
Please turn and look at me.
Your silence causes violence,
I can't stand it anymore.
If I don't say anything,
this class will be a bore.

I have nothing to say,
but I have no purpose without her.
She is my only one,
I live no longer without her.

I have nothing to say,
but she is my sunshine.
Her eyes glow like the moon,
she could walk on water if she tried.

I have nothing to say,
because she has stolen all the words
from my mouth,
with her beauty.

Why is the sky blue,
Because,
Because why,
Because,
Why won't you tell me?
Because I don't know,
But you are much older than me,
Child I find that I was much wiser
when I knew nothing,
The world around me was full of
imagination,
Full of dreams,
And where did that go?
I'm not sure child

The Wise

Tare through the forest,
jump over the trees,
feel it cooling you are the morning
breeze.

One single light can brighten the night,
just as one hand can rule the land.
But hear what I say,
it doesn't need to be this way.

We are creatures of our own demise,
we spend our days shrouded in lies.
But what's to say one day,
we won't be the ones who are truly wise.

Classless and free,
that's how I want to be.
If you've got extra,
give it to the guy next to ya.
Because one day you might be the one
knocking on the door,
and hope that the rich will give to the
poor,
so all our troubles will be no more.

My fair lady,
sitting on a pedestal.
As if she is a princess,
a princess much greater than I,
and I,
a peasant,
just sitting in the sand,
wishes to be with the fair maiden.
For just a second,

for I would cherish it,
that second,
for a thousand years.
For she is the most high,
Elegant.
Beautiful.
And she is mine.

Moonlight beckons on this starry night,
all of the power is in your sight.
Falling through the fractals you see,
what this world is meant to be.

Into the trenches we must hide,
On the back of the snake we will confide.
By the end of this day we will see through,
what Jim wants us to do.

I am a dragonfly,
watch me fly so high.
No way I'm gonna die,
how could this ever be a lie.

What could this world be,
but a constant fight for we.
Look around and see,
what this world could be.

I'm not lying,
you won't see me crying,
this life is only good for dying.

If only,
I could be with her just another moment,
just a second.

If only,
I could touch her cheek,
as if she were here now.

If only,
I could kiss her again,
because then I would never stop.

I Dare

The fair maiden is on an island so far away,
she's all I think about night and day.
I can't begin to tell you how much I love,
this beautiful women that comes from above.

The hero begins to come into view,
I do believe I am one of the few,
who can even imagine love with the lady.
Her eyes are of the most beautiful way, they
shimmer in the morning light,
as I wait by candle light.
Nobody knows my might,
but the lady in the morning light.
She loves me and I know she's right,
even when I am tested by the moonlight.
It glows bright,
like the might,
of my love,
from above.
She knows the way,
to say,
I love your hair,
and I dare,
you to read this poem

Jerry

The wizard is sitting a top the mountain,
looking down at the small village.
They know not of his power.
He is the owl that sits in a tree,
watching the days float by.
Mind of wisdom, heart of gold,
waiting for the day he can finally be bold.
No one knows he's there,
but watching ever so carefully,
he waits for a moment he might dare,
to save the village from all that might scare.

A dragon flies in ready for a fight,
Nothing seems to stand in his way.
Villagers flee, hiding in the forest.
Drop your weapons, you are no match for the dragons might.

Fire rages, green is turned to black,
I can hear the fire crack.
It bellows through the valley,
followed the dragons smack.
Crushing buildings with his tail,
the village looks lost.

The wizard raises his head to see the devastation,
silently floating down on a cloud,
he descends from the mountain.
"Dragon, leave this place now,
if we fight you shall be the one to bow."
"Wizard your power does not phase me,

stand in front of me and you will be but
a tree,
burnt down with a puff of my breath."
"Fine, we shall do it your way dragon,
I will send you home in a wagon."

Dragon took the first shot,
fire burst from his mouth.
The wizard let out a great shout,
the fire was stopped in it's path.
Dragon had failed to do the math.
Wizard raises his hand to the sky,
"I'm sorry Dragon but you must die."

Empty road ride through the desert,
lone house houses no people.
Mountains in the distance,
look or else you'll miss this.
Fire wheel hides behind a blanket,
it's heat to warm for itself.
Love is all it gives to the Earth,
watching from the sky above.

The gates open and my mind is gone,
looking down I see a board I must get
on.
Green rings glide over grey street,
head in the clouds, to celebrate this
great feat.
Bright lights ride behind, as cation gives
in to love,
riding to meet a girl I think is from
above.
She comes down to meet me at night,

and I ask, "When can we run away and
be alone?"
Just one more night,
and we can leave on our endless flight.

Wake up and the dream begins,
open eyes,
closed mind.
Dead until the end of time.
The people around me can't see,
what this world would be, without the
tree.

Wouldn't it be easier if it was over,
death over life,
beauty tainted by terrible people.
Deep down the fire burns,
to take one's own life.
End it all.
Show the world it has no ground.
I'm done,
this world has lost its fun,
Where is my love?

The Abyss

Lost in this abyss,
I'm trying to find my way through the mist.
In the distance I can see a light,
I have to focus with all my might.

Footstep after footstep I'm afraid I might fall,
the ground is empty, it's the end of it all.
Echoes, sweet strange sounds,
where are they coming from as I look around.

Blind-folded by the tremor,
I can't even remember.
What brought me to this place,
I think this shit was laced.

Comfortably numb,
they must think I'm dumb.
But I'm the king,
I can do anything.

The shadow is drawing near,
he's anything but clear.
Lurking in plain sight,
no one see's his light.

Prod the people,
show them the way,
let them know this could be their last day.

You think you're moving forward,
endlessly moving back,

it may be too late when you realize what
you lack.

But there's still hope.
We can open our eyes,
unmask the disguise,
and bring light to all the lies.

Follow me into battle,
the world we will rattle.
Hooded knights of this shadow fight,
we ride until the dawn is bright.

Angel of the everglades,
show me just a shade,
of your magic beauty.

The ceiling bends upward,
as the face on the wall melts,
dripping all over the pelts.
A shaman rises from the ground,
his message makes it around
the circle of indians sitting on the floor,
who are trying to find the door.
"Break on through!" the shaman yells,
just listen you can hear the bells.
The gates are open, almost there,
run with me if you dare.
We're almost there.
Run if you dare.

Under the silver maple I begin to dream,
about a life with a Cajun Queen.
Hair of silk, words of fire,
she's my type of live wire.
Dream is all I may,
I can never think of what to say.
And I await the day,
you say yes, no to all the rest.
I and I is all you need,
and just a little bit of weed.
For you see I am a Jedi,
and that's why, I
am tripping so hard over you.

Snow covered streets hide the broken glass,
pain, anguish,
love, release, evermore.
Walking we see nothing but tracks,
places we once were.
Look up, see the sky,
millions of white warriors,
falling, rejoicing.
Waiting to be stomped out on the sidewalk,
part of the pack,
they have each other's back.
You're looking down again,
afraid to fall.
Don't worry, it's only ice.
Skate be free,
no one can say no.

.

Inspiration

This is my will, a testament to it all,
I want to say in the end Babylon won't fall,
but I know it's just another brick in the wall.
You'd be wrong to say I'm not chasing the ball,
because in the end I'm doing it all.

Inspiration is key now-a-days,
It's the only way you can ride the waves,
find the truth as it lays,
it's inspiration for us to live this way.
I can't sit by another day,
and watch this on going play.

We've taken this world and made it bare,
and all I want to do is declare a dare.
To all those who decide to wear,
their heart on a sleeve and don't care.
You know this life isn't fair,
but when do I see you swear.
Just sit back in your chair,
and listen to this beat blare.

There's nowhere I'd rather be,
but giving inspiration to you and me.
This music will set you free,
look up and see,
that I am the liberator of we,
and this music will set you free.

It's a long road we're on,
chasing after our dreams.
The world bites back,
it isn't what it seems.

A leap of faith into a world unknown,
all because I don't want to die cold and
alone.
She's a beautiful lioness to all who see,
her prowling walk is more than amazing
to me.

Inspiration is key now-a-days,
it's the only way you can ride the waves,
find the truth as it lays,
it's inspiration for us to live this way.
I can't sit by another day,
and watch this on going play.

Love me baby!
I'm coming to get you,
do what ever I have to do love you baby.
Fly across the world to be in your arms.

No need for alarm,
you're mine and I need to claim you,
I can only live without you for a few.
We can run away when you get older,
run away so our love can grow bolder.

The Disease

The man in the black hood,
seems to always do good.
Even with a bounty on his head,
you think he'd surely be dead.

Revolution is his disease,
only the people he cares to please.
The rich man stands with a frown,
he's lost his control over the town.

Clouded pink skies, endlessly roll by,
and I sit here and wonder why,
no one wants to fly high.

One day Babylon will fall,
they will drop the ball.
Make way for the small axe,
don't sit back and relax.

Take the throne,
thrash the castle,
we'll be there with little hassle.

There's nowhere to run from my mind,
I just have to sit here and unwind.
Pillows of white, skies of gold,
this wave is starting to get old.

We're going to light the fire,
stand back it's a live wire.
Never gonna let this die,
I want to see them try.

Never Ending Day

Yes I say,
this is a beautiful day.
Just go out and play,
on this never ending day.

The sun is shinning,
the clouds are floating by.
The sky has no end,
Now spread your wings and fly.

A warm breeze brushes our hair,
embrace it if you dare.
There is nowhere to hide from the sun,
because without him we are done.

Get up and say,
this is a wonderful day.
Nothing can stop us now,
just wipe the sweat from your brow.

Work hard and don't give up,
be as rambunctious as a pup.
This work will bring you glory in the end,
because everyone around you is your friend.

My Hair

As I sit here in this chair,
all I can do is stare.
At the beautiful lady so elegant and fair,
as she tells me a dare.
I should cut off all my hair,
but I sit and swear,
as my head becomes bare.
I've lost the great mane of a mare,
but I think it's fair,
because at the end of the dare,
I shall donate my hair.
So I don't care,
it will be for someone else to wear.

No Disguise

Words they travel on rainbows across
the sea,
to my dear love who idly waits for me.

Stand fast now,
I'm on my way.
So we can run away,
on this perfect day.

There is no disguise,
in your beautiful eyes.
Love burns deep down,
as we lay on the ground.

Arm and arm,
hand and hand,
superheroes, rulers of our land.

Let me hear the lioness rawr,
and we can wage an all out war.
Bodies on bodies we will roll around,
until we end up on the ground.

They

Do they know not what they do?
The victim is strong in them.
Why me? Why me?
Well look around and realize,
you are but one small organism on this
massive plant.
Take grace in your existence.
Don't take it out on another.
Just because you are better off gives you
no right to belittle your brother.
What is to say you won't be in their
shoes one day.
Complaining gets you nowhere.
Why does something so small bring
such great frustration?
They have everything,
so one piece out of place is like the end
of the world to the human race,
but for them we don't matter,
only them.
They say I and I stand alone,
my problems are much greater than
yours.
And at that moment they are struck
down from the heavens,
never to know the true bliss of life.

Herd the pigs,
gather them up.
They follow the leader,
and never know what's up.

Mindless animals on an endless quest,
there lives are meaningless,
no more than the rest.

Wisdom is the mark of experience

We destroy our world and think
nothing of it,
in our minds we're above it.
We watch the world and wonder,
who will step up to the plate and fix our
blunder.

The Queen

Where are you?
We need to leave in a few.
Here comes the morning dew,
changing the world's view.

I see some friends over there,
waiting here is hare to bare.
All I can do is sit and stare,
at the Queen's beautiful hair.

Flowing locks of shimmering gold,
it makes her look so bold.
I sit here and grow old,
as my chances begin to fold.

Prowling lioness of this great land,
why won't you give me your hand.
Our love doesn't need a brand,
your logic is hard to understand.

If you think this is fake,
then you might as well ride the snake,
through the trench, to the lake,
until you finally awake.

Your eyes are portals to the everglades,
they are the perfect shade,
of a color never before made.

www.ingramcontent.com/pod-product-compliance
Lightning Source LLC
Chambersburg PA
CBHW070039070426
42449CB00012BA/3100